Woman to Woman:

It's Time to Change the Game

The Play Book

Authored By: Tanisha Brooks

Woman to Woman:

It's Time to Change the Game

The Play Book

Tanisha Brooks

Precious Pearl Publishing

P.O. Box 1166

Hammond, In. 46325

Copyright © 2010 by Tanisha Brooks

PCN 2010912340

ISBN: 978-0-615-39716-0

Acknowledgements

I cannot thank anyone without first thanking God. Thank you Lord. Thank you for wisdom, inspiration, and for answering prayers.

I'd also like to thank my mommy, Antoinette Davis, who is a constant light in my life. You always shine radiance on me when I'm doing right and reflecting you and God. And like a good mother, you always dim the light whenever necessary and point out my shortfalls when I am not at my best. Thank you for *passing*, shaping, and molding me from your inquisitive little girl to your determined daughter.

Devon Davis, you are my oldest sibling and whether you know it or not I love you dearly. I admire your caring heart and compassionate nature; don't ever change.

Brandon Davis, stay motivated and driven as God sees all. Your hard work and efforts will not go unrewarded.

Denae Davis, as sisters we have our ups and downs which are inevitable, but as sisters nothing and no one can come between our bond. We have fought tough, laughed hard, and partied harder. I don't know about you; but, I still got some partying left in me. Next time around let's promise to party smarter.

We don't always see eye to eye and we probably never will; but Bertha Brooks, grandma keep being you. I wouldn't trade your strong will for anything in the world. I love you.

Thank you Richard Davis for being more than a stepfather. Every girl needs a daddy; and, I am proud to say I have that in you.

Thank you to my countless family and friends. I have not forgotten anyone.

You and I both know the special place you hold in my heart.

With all that being said, I can't forget those whom this book is dedicated to. Every boyfriend, school yard crush, or man that I've dated, cried over, or checked yes in the box saying I'd go with you, this book couldn't have been written without the imprint you've left on my life. I don't have any harsh feelings or regrets. I thank each and every one of you. I've learned so much; and because of you I have firsthand knowledge and many experiences to share, cheers!

Play List

Warm Up

The Game Done Changed

Dilemma

I do not wish to be single my entire life. When I was a little girl I dreamed of having the American Dream when I became a *young* adult. The dream was to be married, have children, along with living in a big pretty house with a two car garage and picket fence. I have held on to that dream. And because I am an optimist, I believe that I will still become a wife and live happily in my big, pretty, well decorated home. As for the children, I'm in my thirties; and, with no significant prospects of a husband in near sight, neither are children.

Of course, I have options. I can become yet another single black mother, raising a daughter. A mother unable to give her the self love and respect that is obtained when dually raised by a supportive father, who is the one man able to truly show her just how valuable she is. Or, I can have a son and give him all the motherly love I have to offer, but never teach or show him how to be a man. Because truth of the matter is only a man can teach a boy how to be one. Don't get me wrong. I am not knocking the countless single mothers who get up daily, bust their butts to put food on tables, clothes on backs, and shoes on feet. I am simply choosing not to take on that role alone.

It would be possible to give up and point the blame at myself concluding something must be wrong with me. After all, I am the one who hasn't reached my dream. But I see similar instances of my own circumstance far too often in my work, at church, in my community, and within my family. So I'm left asking myself the question; are *our* dreams a lost cause? Should we go to bed at night and abandon those dreams atop our pillows when we awake? I would like to think abandonment is not an option. I would like to think that if I'm able to bare witness to a Black man in the white house I can most certainly be a wife with a Black man in my house.

The Way Things Used To Be

On numerous instances I've had conversations with female friends and we've asked, concerning dating and relationships, what happened to the way things used to be?

- What happened to men opening doors and pulling out chairs?
- What ever happened to flowers and candy before a date?
- What happened to dinner, a movie, then saying goodnight with a hug at the door?
- Hell, whatever happened to dates?

I can remember a time, not so long ago, when it was a given that after meeting a man, a date would soon follow. Even if this man was a so called player, and had no intentions on developing a serious relationship or commitment, a date most certainly preceded any expectation of physical contact. Then, over night, it seemed as if a secret memo had been sent to all men, informing them women no longer required the customary introductory song and dance. After exchanging numbers, during the first phone call, men began to ask questions like, "Can I come over and keep you company or sit on your couch and watch TV with you?" The assumption has already been made that I am desperate and/or foolish enough to let a complete stranger come to my house without ever even meeting publically on a casual basis for so much as an ice cream cone.

Upon this revelation I asked myself two things. "Am I the only woman who no longer warrants dates; or, is it the type of man I'm attracted to who no longer dates?" I'm inquisitive by nature, so I began to listen when other women were talking around the office, hair dryers, manicure tables, and the like. I concluded for the most part, at least one date was no longer a prerequisite to a relationship or sex, no matter the type of man.

But what I found most surprising during my informal research is that women were accepting and going along with this foreign manner. They were entering relationships as if standards were non existent by choice and as if choices were no longer an option. I do not believe the entering of dateless, one-sided, unhealthy relationships is a woman's desire because complaints from women concerning men's behavior are at an all time high. Perhaps the disconnect between the way a relationship is entered and the way it plays out is not apparent to some women, but the disconnect is crystal clear to me.

Time Out:

Disclaimer: While reading, some women will become upset which is expected. Oftentimes the truth is difficult to accept. I speak from the heart; and, when the truth comes from the heart, what's best is to open up and be accepting so growth may take place.

I have also been known to be harsh, blunt, and to the point. In other words, I keep it straight, no chaser and refuse to put cherries and sugar on top of crap. I am by no means a relationship expert or marriage counselor. My qualifications include having in the past made, and eye witnessed, many of the mistakes mentioned in this book. With that being said,

keep an open mind and continue at your own risk.
But don't ever say, I didn't warn you!

Resume Warm Up

I'll cut right to the chase. I see no need to beat around the bush, pulling you along on a string, in order for you to find out why I believe we have lost our power. As I see it, the only reason a woman would allow herself to be treated less than what she deserves is because she is desperate and/or feels a sense of inadequacy.

Somewhere along the way women have lost their sense of self worth. If you don't feel worthy you begin to show your lack of value: by what you'll allow; the way you behave; how you carry yourself; dress, walk, and talk. Similar activities take place when a person is desperate. A desperate woman will lose herself trying to obtain what she thinks she wants by settling for less and putting others above herself.

Now you may be thinking that neither of the two describes you. But I can almost guarantee that if you've dated in the last few years, keep reading and you'll find some similarities in your recent relationships, the relationships of girlfriends, or loved ones, and instances described in this book.

Why Don't Men Act Right?

Whenever I meet a man the first thing he wants to know is why someone as attractive as me, appearing to have it going on in every aspect of my life, is single. Most often my answer is simply, "Because men don't act right." Of course, the next logical questions posed are, "What do you mean men don't act right? – How do you expect to be treated?" Quite frankly these questions annoy the hell out of me, because I am convinced every man young and old knows just how to act. They all know how to behave and treat a woman; they just choose not to do so. Truth of the matter is... **I can't blame them**.

Why would a man choose to date me, take his time getting to know me *before becoming physical*, when every other woman is making things far too simple for him? I and others like myself have become more than a chase. We are a notion of the past, a nuisance, with standards that simply no longer need be applied. I am flexible. But I do not, and will not, choose to settle or conform to the lowered standards of today.

However, the optimist in me will make a plea, a call to action if you will, to all women. Please stand up, and reclaim your power! Unfortunately, only a handful of women, myself included, are unable to make the needed change on our own. While standing strong as a united front, I see no reason women of today can't recover their role as mother *and* wife, regain respect, and most of all their POWER!

Play One

It Begins Within

How many times have you heard someone say you must love yourself before expecting someone else to? There is a lot of truth to be found in this saying. You must love yourself before seeking a relationship. If not, you will find yourself used and repeatedly walked on or taken advantage of. You will begin to settle, attracting men who prey on vulnerable women. Men, like predators, can smell vulnerability and fear a mile away. You'll be wondering why you keep attracting the same type of man. You keep attracting the same type of guy because you are giving off the aroma of weak and timid, the stench of inadequacy and insufficiency. This unfortunately for you either smells like a free ride to a free loader or has the look of a supple bone to a dog.

Play One, First Down

Take power over your life.

After all it's your life. Who better to control it than you? Decide what you want to do, and simply do it. Abandon all excuses. Excuses hold you back and keep you from becoming the best woman you can possibly be. The finest most well put together man wants a beautiful (inwardly and outwardly) well put together woman.

Power is sexy and commands authority. A woman of power walks into a room with confidence. She does not need to be loud or make a scene to gain attention. Attention is sought due to her mere presence. Like life support men will seek to find what she has as if their very last breath is depending on it.

Because she knows this a powerful woman does not need to overcompensate or compete with other women. Other women are your teammates not your opponents. Ladies, in order to win we must be team players. Although getting a man may seem like a competition, in order to be taken seriously and have your expectations met, approach relationships in a non competitive, no nonsense manner. By doing so you are telling a man I am not a toy; so, don't play with me. He will know that if he is serious about you he needs to trade in his player card, and start applying his A game. He will acknowledge you have become the starting player and all others can be benched until further notice.

Play One, Second Down

Find out what makes you happy.

Lack of happiness indicates a void. First, find the source of the void and fill it. If you are not happy you should not look for happiness in someone else. True happiness comes from within. If you are unsure of what you're lacking, try making a list of everything you are not currently pleased with. Exclude all things pertaining to a man, relationship, or people in general. List the steps one by one you need to fix to rid you of your unhappiness. Then begin filling the void step by step. Take baby steps if need be, as long as you are moving towards your ultimate goal, happiness. A sample list is provided.

I am unhappy with my current life situation:

1. First thing Monday morning, I will apply to at least five jobs with higher paying salaries.

2. Seek a real estate agent or apartment guide and begin to narrow in on the area I'd like to move.

3. I will save x amount of dollars each pay period by cutting out frivolous spending.

4. In six months I will be living in my ideal home.

Whatever your goal may be, the point is to write your goals and begin to work on them one at a time until they are fully achieved.

Play One, Third Down

Make improvements.

We feel better about ourselves when we believe we are at our best. When people feel they are at their best they position themselves around similar individuals. When we feel good about ourselves we begin to feel deserving and expecting better treatment from others. This is essential to regaining your power.

Physical improvements are always a good place to start. Always, always, look your best, even if just making a quick run to the store. You never know what old friend you're going to run into or new friend you're going to meet. Get a new hairstyle that is up to date and compliments you well. Treat yourself to manicures, pedicures, and massages as often as you can.

If you can't afford to go to the salon or spa to have professional care buy a kit and do the treatments at home yourself. Or perhaps you and your girlfriend or daughter can get together and do one another weekly. Another great option is finding a school that offers spa services. They often offer cheaper rates with the same quality of service.

Buy a new outfit that flatters your shape. After all, you deserve it. If you can't afford a new outfit get together with a group of girlfriends and have exchange parties, giving away older gently used pieces. Don't pack up a bunch of trash and take to your friends. Take the things you still like and would wear if you had the perfect accessories. The rule is, if you haven't worn it in two years, get rid of it. This way you have room for the things you will wear.

If you feel the need to lose a few pounds take power and begin to work towards your goal. If need be, start off slowly. Take a daily walk. Go dancing. Go roller skating. Be creative; there are countless ways to become active, lose weight, and still have fun.

Try not to diet. Make healthy eating a part of your lifestyle. Try eating your last meal by six o'clock in the evening. I'm not saying deprive yourself of all the pleasures fried foods and chocolate have to offer. But just think of the pleasures that come from looking and feeling your best. Ask yourself, would I rather have a piece of pie, or be a dime piece? Once you begin to see results you'll gain momentum and the motivation needed to push harder and maintain.

If you're seeking a better job, promotion, or you've always wanted to return to school, there is no better time than the present. Make a list of your goals. Take the easiest one or two, and begin working on those first. Try teaming up with a friend. Write your goals, put them inside an envelope, then exchange envelopes. Six months down the line, mail the envelopes, and see how many of your goals you've accomplished.

The bottom line is you know what is plaguing and holding you down. Let's stop blaming ourselves and others for dreams deferred. Whatever the previous obstacle(s) they are all irrelevant now. So let's make them a thing of the past by eliminating hurdles so that you fulfill your hearts desires.

The skies the limit; so, remember not to sell yourself short. I know it sounds cliché; but, you can do and be anything you set your mind to. Don't let insecurities stand in your way; and, do not let others negative outlooks get the best of you.

Play One, Fourth Down

Surround yourself with positive supportive people.

Ever hear the saying, birds of a feather flock together? When you surround yourself with positive people their optimistic behavior begins to rub off on you. Positivity breeds positivity. When you put positive energy in the air, like a magnet, you pull positive things your way. When you are releasing negativity (bad attitude, rude behavior, and the like) the same occurs. Your world (career, friendships, relationships etc.) begin to crumble when surrounded by negativity; and, you never seem to get ahead or obtain the joy you're looking for.

You are a reflection of your thoughts. When you think negatively, bad karma and misfortune surround you. Ever notice the person who's always talking about how broke they are and how they don't have any money? Ever notice how true their statement is? They *are* always broke; they *don't* ever have any money. This is so because they are constantly telling the universe I don't have anything. In turn, they don't attract financial blessings.

This scenario holds true in every situation. Therefore, speak positivity into your life. Try repeating affirmations. "I have all the things I want and need." You'll begin to notice, by repeating this statement your situation will turn around and positive good fortune will come your way.

Supportive people are those that help build you up not try to tear you down. They want what's best for you. They do not want to see you stuck in the same place, or think it's all right for you to move ahead as long as you remain two steps behind them. They are not jealous or envious of you and your achievements. They do not want to see you stuck in the same dead end relationship, job, or other circumstance. They have your best interests at heart. Positive supportive people will help motivate, and keep you on the right track to obtaining happiness. Imagine the President being married to someone who told him his dreams were too large.

I have a friend who was in a long term relationship since high school. She went on to receive her bachelor's then master's degree. Meanwhile, her boyfriend seemed to be complacent and didn't strive to achieve similar goals. He didn't receive secondary education and therefore, was unable to move ahead in his career; and, his earning potential became capped. My friend decided she wanted to enroll in a doctorate program. He began to belittle her telling her that she was looking to become a career student and was afraid of the real world. What he was actually trying to tell her is, "I am envious of your success and my ego can't take anymore!"

Male pride is one of the worst things to have to deal with which is why we are more compatible with like minded individuals. My friend out grew her relationship and it was time to move on. My view is one should avoid non supportive people like the plague.

Play One, Fifth Down

End negative cycles and generational curses.

Ever hear the sayings, "Don't be like me. Be better than me; or, do as I say not as I do?" Don't make all the same mistakes family members have made in the past. Take mistakes you saw growing up and turn them into learning experiences.

So often we try to mask the obvious and hide the apparent. Recognize bad advice and run in the other direction. A former co worker and friend was in a dead end relationship. Five years deep, it was going absolutely nowhere and she was being taken advantage of in every sense imaginable. Her family members would tell her things like: *you know he loves you; he's just a man and doesn't know how to show it. When he's ready, he'll give you a ring."* Wouldn't you know it, not even a year after their final breakup his new fiancé was expecting.

Play Two

Don't Settle

Before entering a relationship remember the African Proverb, "Before you get married keep both eyes open; once you're married close one eye." No one has ever become internally peaceful by settling. Yes, things might look great on the outside or on paper. Your man's happiness may be achieved. But when you settle, you're telling yourself you are undeserving and do not warrant the best. This in turn is exactly what happens. You're only going to get as much as you expect to receive. So expect the best and that's what you'll get!

Play Two, First Down

Look out for numero uno.

Determine your wants, needs, and desires in a man. Make a list. As with saying affirmations, by writing down and rereading your wants you start to internalize them and they begin to take on a life of their own, materializing and actually happening. A sample list appears below.

My Man Is...

1. Single
2. Humble
3. Clean
4. God Fearing
5. Attentive
6. Respectful
7. Thoughtful
8. Ambitious
9. Supportive
10. Kind Hearted
11. Faithful
12. Honest
13. Etc

Your list should include all the qualities you desire in a partner. List everything you can think of. As time goes on build your list. Remember that when you read your list aloud believe what you're saying. You can and will attract all you want as long as you believe your desires are attainable!

Don't talk yourself into believing you don't deserve everything you want. Sometimes our insecurities get in the way of our obtaining all that we are capable of achieving and receiving. When it comes to choosing a man know that you deserve someone who possesses all the qualities you're looking for as well as one's you didn't even realize you wanted!

Date men who possess these qualities. If you're dating someone who doesn't possess these attributes you'll end up unhappy in the end. There is a difference between what you want and what you need and should not tolerate. Remember, we **all** have imperfections. Small quirks that are not big deals may be overlooked. So what, he sleeps in the middle of the bed instead of on his side. Cuddle up to him. Big deal, he watches Monday night football faithfully. Read a book, watch a movie, or catch up on _____ (fill in the blank).

On the other hand, some things are deal breakers. If you prefer a man without kids, who works, won't smoke, doesn't drink, curse, or goes to church every Sunday you don't have to bend. Don't overlook warning signs when dating. When you overlook important qualities those same things you overlooked in the beginning are the ones that'll haunt your relationship when things begin to get difficult. You'll resent your man when in fact, you should be upset with yourself for getting involved with someone you knew wasn't right for you from the start.

Oftentimes you'll hear people tell highly accomplished women it's okay to date men who aren't yet accomplished because of their nice, nurturing, or sensitive nature. This is code for settle or lower your standards. This is a novel idea for younger couples who are both just getting established. In other few and far between instances, which are most often the exception and not the rule.

When a man sees a woman who he isn't really attracted to his friends don't encourage pursuit by telling him, "Work with her man, I can see potential." No, they look at what is being presented at the moment.

Is it fair for you to work hard doing whatever you had to do, to get where you are today, to be with someone you have to continually pull to keep pace with you? If you're both in your thirties, forties, or older you must ask yourself what he's been doing all this time. Quite possibly you'll always be pulling him along. If he hasn't mustered up the ambition to obtain anything in the 10, 15, perhaps even 20 or so years since high school, what makes you think he's going to all of a sudden do it now; because you came along? I think not. Chances are he's a person who just talks a good game. Ladies, it's time to change the game. Like the perfect shoes for an outfit, let's choose men who complement us well.

You don't need to try to change a man into something he's not. "Fixing a man up" is selfish. How would you like someone trying to change you into his dream woman? How would you like a man telling you how to wear your hair, dress, talk, eat, what to watch, where to go? Get the point? It wouldn't be fair to you; and, it isn't right when we do it either. Instead, be patient and find the man you're actually looking for who doesn't need you to fill in for his mother, barber, tailor or the like. He is out there.

Realize there is nothing wrong with you having standards and sticking to them. Don't be ashamed of what you want. You don't need a good reason or excuse to validate your likes and preferences. You don't need to date someone out of pity. Mr. Potentiality, Mr. In Between, and Mr. Right Now will all find women who truly don't mind their quirks, and so will you.

Be honest with men. If you aren't into him, don't string him along. Treat men the same as you desire to be treated. The negative treatment you inflict upon others has a way of showing its ugly head at your doorstep. Ever hear of karma? How would you like to meet the man of your dreams and things don't work out because you're being repaid for doing someone wrong in the past? The idea is to change the game, not start playing a whole new game whose rules imply that we lie, cheat, and deceive to score points.

Play Two, Second Down

Slow down.

How many times have you found yourself single wishing for and wanting nothing more than to be in a relationship? You look at your girlfriends and co workers and either secretly or outwardly desire what they have. You pray and prey for it. Destiny fulfilled; you finally receive it. Things are going great as they most often do in the beginning of relationships. All of a sudden all hell seems to break lose. You begin to truly learn who this dream man is. It turns out that he is not a dream after all, but a nightmare. You look back longingly at your single days remembering the carefree bliss which accompanied them.

Take your time. Get to truly know and understand the person you're dating before committing yourself to a relationship. When initially meeting someone it's an introduction. They will show you bits and pieces of who they actually are as time progresses. As time passes the more you'll find out and be exposed to the real personality. Some of what is shown to you, you'll like and enjoy. Other parts of their personality you can do without or want to run far away from. The goal is not to turn an obvious *brick* into your new beau. This is the blessing that comes with taking your time and slowly brewing relationships.

Despite what we think, we don't always know what's best for us. The best things do come to those who wait; so, hold out for what you really want. As the old saying goes, *we don't always get the things we want and need when we want them; but, they always have a funny way of coming right on time.*

As a rule of thumb, take time to heal between relationships. As time passes we are able to recognize mistakes made and learn from them. Jumping from relationship to relationship doesn't allow sufficient time needed for healing or self reflection. We go through trials in order to learn life's lessons. If the needed lessons haven't been learned, we continue to make the same mistakes. How can we ever move along and get ahead if we remain stuck in the same place? We must look at failed relationships as blessings. We should know we are moving closer to what God has waiting for us.

It's okay to have a closet full of bags, not baggage. You do not want to carry excess baggage around with you. Baggage weighs heavy on the backs of children, family, and future romantic relationships. Children watch and mimic knowingly and unknowingly everything we say and do. Therefore, always be mindful of what you say, do, and who you bring around children. Every man you meet or go out with is not someone you'd want to introduce to your child. Children are very impressionable and we must make sure the men we bring into their lives make good impressions. By taking time with relationships and dating, you get to learn who this guy is **before** bringing him around your children.

Play Two, Third Down

Take no prisoners.

If you are not receiving all you want, expect, and deserve from your relationship it is best you let your partner know. After said discussion, sit back, and wait for change. He needs to let you know through his actions that he's heard your wishes; and, his desire is to make you happy by meeting your expectations.

If you've told your live in boyfriend you'd like, after a night of partying with the guys, he returns home at a sensible hour or before 2:00 a.m., and he does not adhere to your reasonable request, give him a dose of his own medicine. Do not remind him of your previous request; *trust me he has not forgotten.* The following weekend proceed to get dressed to a tee. Perhaps, wear *his* favorite outfit, and let him know you're going out with the girls so don't wait up. If and when he calls your cellphone hearing loud music and laughter in the background, let him know you can hardly hear what he's saying; and, you will talk to him when you get in. Do not ruin your night out with your cell phone glued to your ear as this was not the case when you were home alone. Turn your phone off then proceed to have the time of your life. Your man will be okay because certainly what he dishes he can receive.

Similarly, I previously found myself in a new live-in relationship. My man was suffering from the case of "I miss my homies syndrome". While hanging out, he decided he'd rather spend the night out with the guys, instead of coming home at a reasonable hour which had been clearly established at the beginning of our relationship.

He, like many men, in order to steer the attention away from his wrong doing, phoned and picked an irrelevant argument. He then proceeded to ask if I'd mind packing his things and having them ready when he picked them up the next morning. Needless to say, I was crushed. Despite my hurt feelings, and unlike most women, I did not sit home and cry all night, then the next day let him come in, and sweet talk me out of my panties and back into his place to stay. Unlike some instances, game recognized game. I got up, neatly packed all of his things, put on my "freak him" girl dress with the side split that ought to be against the law. I then drove to where he was hanging out. Gave him all his items and informed him in an ever so lady like manner that since I was in the area I saw no need for him to make an unnecessary trip the following day. I then got back in my car, turned off my already ringing cell phone, drove back home, and went to bed. And instead of crying myself to sleep, I laughed myself to sleep. *Well done. Two points for the home team.*

If attempts one and two have been made to no avail, it is best you start making decisions of your own concerning your worth, your best interest, and what you will and will not tolerate. There is simply no reason to continue to nag someone about the same thing, time and time again. Either he is going to change or he isn't. Either you can tolerate the situation or you can't. He has already determined you're going to actually do something about it or you're not; and, nagging does not make you more appealing.

Play Two, Fourth Down

The *trip*, not the *trick* to the alter.

On more than a couple of instances I've witnessed friends in long term relationships longing for marriage or children, nagging their partner to fulfill their dream. Once the relationship finally dissipates, not so surprisingly, six months to a year later, the woman is distraught. She's heard her is now expecting a child with someone else, engaged, or already married. Do not allow yourself to be strung along. Either get what you want or leave; but, don't settle.

Likewise, if you have been with a man for three or more years and marriage is your ultimate goal, you need to realize this man who claims he isn't ready for marriage, in most instances, is just not going to marry you. Ask yourself, "do I want to marry a man who isn't thrilled about the prospect of spending the rest of his life with me?" I don't know about you, but when I go to sleep at night I want to know the man I'm laying next to is there because he wants to be there, not because I tricked him to the alter.

Just face it, if he's not ready for what you're ready for, after the walk down the aisle, things aren't magically going to be perfect. Marriage is difficult enough without being married to someone who isn't ready for, or doesn't want that type of commitment. Be glad your guy is telling you he isn't ready to take the plunge. Thank him for saving you plenty of unnecessary heartbreak and headache.

Some might ask the question how long is too long to wait for a serious commitment, engagement, or walk down the aisle. The answer is; it depends. Every situation is different. Some couples weren't dating seriously when they first met; and, a longer courtship may be necessary in these circumstances. Other couples are young. I don't particularly believe in people marrying before they've had an opportunity to experience life. Older mature adults, who have experienced life and its lessons, tend to know what they're looking for and when they've found it, sooner than younger couples. If this is the case, your guy should know by the second year if you're what he considers, "wife material." If he can't make the decision, make it for him and leave. Don't waste countless years waiting on someone to realize your worth.

Play Two, Fifth Down

It is what it is.

People don't always say what's on their mind. Sometimes, we must read actions and take hints to determine the unspoken. Simply put, an interested person acts interested. One way a man will show his interest in you is by the time he's willing to commit. Men like to use the excuse I don't have time to do this or that because I keep a very busy schedule. People in general, make time for whatever they want to make time for. If you're a priority, you won't miss him because he won't let you.

Unfortunately, more often than not, men won't tell us verbally when they aren't interested, no longer care, or no longer wish to be in a relationship. Instead, most tend to take the easy way out and begin to slowly pull away. This action should not be considered a game of tug of war. If he begins to pull away, do not use your strength and energy trying your hardest to pull him closer in your direction. This action causes him to run further from you. If he is desperately trying to yank the relationship rope from your grasp, let it go completely. Let him fall back. He will either get up, realizing playing your game is a winning hand, or run completely out of your grasp. In either case, you win. The object of the game is to be with someone who actually wants to be with you. You do not *hack* to score points, attempting to trap the uninterested.

Have you ever noticed; the more unattracted and uninterested you are in a man, the more attracted and interested in you he becomes? The same is true for men. Even if a man is genuinely interested in you in the beginning, oftentimes we run men away by being too available, needy, and way too transparent. My motto is treat the guy you're head over heels for the same as you'd treat the guy you're just not in to.

Do not let wanting a relationship or spouse consume you or your dating experiences. I have a very close girlfriend who desperately wants to be married. Every man she meets she strategically interviews to see if he's marriage material. If not, she no longer dates him and totally looks in the other direction.

Ladies, dating is supposed to be fun. There is no fun in going on an interview disguised as a date. So what, he isn't Mr. Right. Date with an open mind. He may not be Mr. Right, but he may be Señor New Best friend or Mr. Something to do on the Weekend.

Remember, every man you meet or go out with is not your future husband. Every man you're attracted to will not be attracted to you. Nor, will every man you want to pursue something more serious with view you in the same regard. Adapt the motto, some will, some won't, so what, next!

The bottom line is, we cannot be afraid of being alone. When you are afraid you begin to lose your power. Being alone is only what you make it and being alone and lonely are two totally different things. Being alone does not have to be a bad situation; so embrace solitude. It is a time for self reflection, empowerment, and improvement. Reflect on past relationships. Learn from mishaps and focus on making improvements so that you do not become a repeat offender. There is nothing worse than a person who repeatedly makes the same mistakes, over and over, time and time again.

Remember the bible story of Moses leading the Israelites from a life of slavery to the Promised

Land?   The journey to the Promised Land from Pharaoh was a three day trip; a three day journey that took the Israelites seven years to make. As a pastor similarly preached in a sermon, do not live life like the Israelites, going around and around in circles wasting precious time, when your Promised Land (Man) is within reaching range.

When relationships aren't going as we'd like or as expected, after so long, we must be strong and face realizations. As my mother would say, "Put your big girl draws on." Cry yourself a river, draw yourself a bridge, and get over it.

Validate Yourself! You have worth and value alone or with a man; therefore, you don't need a man to validate your worth. You are good single. As a couple you should be great. Ask yourself:

- If this man isn't adding value or worth to my already high stock, why do I need him?

- If my man constantly takes and never gives, why is he here?

- If I am not doing better with him, than I was without him, why am I with him?

A woman was once in a grocery store and ran into an old friend. They chatted for a while catching up on old times. She told her friend of her marriage and three children. Her friend reciprocated sharing her own family stories. They made promises to keep in touch, but life has a funny way of evolving and they were never able to reconnect.

Five years later, the women happened to run into each other again. The friend immediately walked up to the woman, wearing a broad smile embraced her and said, "Look at you girl! You must have left your husband." The moral of the story...no woman should change outwardly, while in a relationship, to the extent that it is possible to glance at her and tell, that the relationship has ended.

Play Three

Expect Respect

If you find that you are unhappy with your relationship more often than you are happy, than perhaps you need to reexamine your relationship. If a man truly loves and cares about you, he does not break you and tear you down physically, verbally, or emotionally. In contrast, he builds your self-esteem; because a man that cares will want to see you happy.

When you love someone you want the best for them in every sense of the word. He does not want harm to come your way no matter the source. The African Proverb states, "Woman was taken out of man; not out of his head to top him, nor out of his feet to be trampled underfoot; but, out of his side to be equal to him, under his arm to be protected, and near his heart to be loved."

Play Three, First Down

Don't Be a Pushover.

I'm not saying be pompous and rude, but no one likes a push over. Men respect women who have opinions, are able to stand up for themselves, and won't tolerate being pushed over. You do not need to be afraid of his reaction to your opposition. In a mutually respectful relationship, he will be mindful of your likes and dislikes. So, feel free to speak your mind and give your opinion.

If your guy asks for your opinion, it's because he wants it. Don't tell him what you think he wants to hear just to appease him. No, people don't want their feelings hurt when they ask a question. But what ends up happening when you answer truthfully is, he respects you for being strong enough to be honest.

Ever have a friend whom you call when you want an honest opinion on a complex situation, or even a new hairstyle, or outfit? You call on that particular friend because you know their opinion will be honest, rather it hurts or not. Men respect the same honesty in a partner. Be strong and speak your mind. In the end, everyone ends up happy.

If a situation arises in which you are unpleased with the way your guy has chosen to handle it, speak up immediately. Do not wait until resentment has built to bring up the matter. People tend to respect you most when you put them in their place immediately. You must teach people how to treat you. Let others know right off what is, and is not acceptable, and what will, and will not be tolerated.

For example, if a guy forgets to call when he said he would, speak on the issue when you do finally hear from him. Let him know you expect him to follow through when he says he's going to do something. Don't wait until it builds up and he has done it repeatedly. By this time, you've trained him to believe it is okay to say one thing to you, and do the opposite.

I know a guy who was in a relationship in which he was verbally abusive and completely disrespectful. After the abusive relationship ended he pursued a new relationship. In the new relationship he showed none of the previous demeaning characteristics. The difference between the two relationships is not the guy, but how the woman carried the herself. The first girlfriend was always available, needy, and fragile. The new girlfriend was available when it was good for her. She showed independence, and strength. She was not afraid to lose him or the relationship and therefore, spoke her mind and put her foot down whenever uncomfortable situations or unpleasant behaviors presented themselves. The new girlfriend basically taught this guy to respect her and treat her the way she wished to be treated.

Moreover, there is a way in which your partner should speak to you, in public, and behind closed doors. Some things are best said while alone in the comfort of your own home. Fronting you off, in front of others is a sign of immaturity, lack of respect, or he simply just doesn't give a _____ about you. In any instance, it does not have to be tolerated.

Play Three, Second Down

Abuse, will not be tolerated.

Again, abuse is abuse, be it physical, verbal or emotional. I do believe that generational curses and learned behavior haunt some men; and, while they know better, they are unable to do better until they get the professional help they need. Sometimes, when we love people we have to be strong, and love ourselves enough to let them go. It is not necessary to stay in an abusive relationship. In fact, if you've found true love, there is no need to be afraid of being apart for a while because true love will find you again when you have both matured.

You need time away as well. You need to work on yourself to find out what is inside you that would cause you to attract and stay with someone who treats you in this manner. *(Reference Chapter 2, It Begins Within)* While in an abusive relationship it is not the time to prove points to yourself or others. Do not consider your failed relationship as defeat. Do not talk yourself into believing that it is your job to stick it out. It is your job to do what's best for you. Submitting yourself to abusive behavior is not beneficial to you and your happiness in any way whatsoever. If people say I told you so tell them you're right, you did; and, keep it moving. The point is not how long it took you to realize you needed to leave; what's important is that you realized it before it was too late. *Goal scored!*

Play Three, Third Down

Love, is not supposed to hurt.

Sometimes people try to make themselves feel better by tearing others down and picking away at their self esteem. This is so because they are lacking internally. Verbal and emotional abuse can leave scars that last much longer than those of physical abuse.

I know a woman, who was in a relationship that was both verbally and emotionally abusive. By the time she finally had enough, and left the relationship, her self esteem was so badly damaged she could not even look a man in the face. It takes strength and courage to leave a situation in which your self-esteem has been badly compromised. Believe and know that no matter how bad things have gotten in the past, they can and will get better. God did not put you here to suffer; and your past does not dictate your future. I know, because that woman wrote this book.

Play Four

Don't Bend Over Backwards

We all have heard the saying do unto others as you would have others do unto you. But, never do more for another person than they are willing to do for you. Treat your man the way you'd like to be treated. But if you're willing to give more than he is, than maybe you don't rank high on his list of priorities.

Play Four, First Down

Don't bend over backwards in the bedroom.

I do not mean this in the literal sense. If you can do back bends, head stands, pole tricks, somersaults and flips, by all means do so; if this is what you wish to do. Naturally, as women, we like to please others. But do not contort yourself into a giver and pleaser, losing you, while trying to gratify others.

If there's an act your man wishes you to perform and you don't want to, don't do it. Chances are if it doesn't feel right to you, it won't feel good to you. My motto is, "If you don't want your grandmother, mother or daughter to do it then don't ask me."

Sure, couples like to be adventurous at times. Spice in the bedroom is what keeps the relationship cooking. But I personally believe if a man truly loves and cares about you, he does not wish to watch, or participate in sexual acts, that involve you and others. A man who cares shows a sense of ownership and pride for the woman he loves. He wants her all to himself.

True enough, he may have fantasies, but most men's wildest fantasies aren't meant to be performed by the women they love. Think about the negative consequences a threesome can have on your relationship. How would you feel if he seems to enjoy the other woman more than he does you? Think about how it'll feel to watch your man have sex with another woman. Sometimes, it is best to put your feelings above others desires. You are a woman, not a Jeanie in a bottle here to grant his every wish and desire. There is nothing wrong with having unfulfilled fantasies; that way he has something to dream about when he goes to sleep.

Play Four, Second Down

Don't bend over backwards in the kitchen.

Trust, there are other ways to a man's heart than through his stomach. Your man is not an adolescent; and, you are not his mother. Unless you are on his payroll, cooking and cleaning for him are not your job responsibilities.

Others tend to take these deeds for granted, especially when you walk through his front door for the first time and begin picking up after him, doing his laundry, and preparing his meals. By taking on these tasks, you give him the idea that you are subservient; and, your role is to cook and clean for him at his beckon call with little gratitude or appreciation, shown by him for your efforts.

Like time, all things change. Traditionally, husbands worked outside the home paying all of the bills and solely financially supporting the family. In turn, the wife tended the children and the indoor household chores (cooking, cleaning, laundry, etc.). Understandably, the traditional duties of wives changed when it became necessary for women to join the workforce in order to monetarily help support the family.

Simply put, if all the adults in the house are working and paying bills, all the adults should contribute to cleaning the house. The manner in which the chores are divvied is up to the couple. But certainly, we can all agree, that if everyone leaves the house daily to work the same amount of hours outside the home, we can put equal amounts of effort into the work that must be done inside the home.

Women should not begin to do things in the beginning of a relationship they do not wish to continue in an effort to snag a man. If you do not wish to be a five star chef, slaving over meals daily, then do not start out this way. Don't get me wrong there are certain exceptions that apply from time to time. If you feel your efforts will be appreciated, then sure, invite him over for dinner. You have to eat anyway. If you are a stay at home girlfriend or wife, and your man leaves the house daily to bring all the bread and bacon into the kitchen, I see nothing wrong with you cooking it. But on the other hand, if working and paying the bills are a dual effort; household chores, preparing and putting home cooked meals on the table should be a dual effort.

Play Four, Third Down

Don't bend over backwards with your finances.

Let a man be a man. He is not your child who depends on your financial support. His bills, clothes, and recreation, are not your financial responsibility. Men are not to be bought or purchased. The man who has to be bought is only yours on borrowed time.

This philosophy applies to cougars as well. If the young man you're entertaining genuinely cares for you, he won't mind paying for dates and doing nice things for you. Generally, when a person cares for you they find ways to show they care by paying for dates and buying other trinkets, or by listening to your needs and administering small gestures.

Real men prefer to be in charge financially. They do not want to feel hen pecked and taken care of. Instead, they enjoy the masculine role and eagerly take on the financial responsibility that comes along with it. This does not mean that the woman never comes out of her pocket. It is more than okay for us to pay for dates, buy gifts, and help pick up financial slack if we're able to. But, what we don't do is apply these gestures in an effort to buy affection. Putting his cell phone, car, flat screen television etc., in your name are not ways of showing your love. Remember, you are beautiful inside and out and what you have to offer is not only wanted by a man, but needed; and, it cannot be found in your wallet. The man that genuinely cares for you will be with you despite what you are able or unable to do for him financially.

Play Four, Fourth Down

Don't bend over backwards for someone who won't bend over backwards for you.

Don't lose yourself while in a relationship. Some women give too much of themselves, and in turn, end up having their efforts go unrewarded and underappreciated. Do not drop everything because your man has shown up. Of course you want to spend time with him. Of course he requires attention; but, the world does not stop spinning when he walks into a room, and neither should yours. If you were on the phone before he walked into the house, finish your phone call; then, tend to him. Every time the phone rings and he's on the other line doesn't mean you have to immediately end your call, to talk to him. Click over and tell him you'll call him back. Don't click over and forget your girlfriend, mom, or whoever was on the other line.

Do not begin to devote all your time and efforts into your man and forget the individual you were prior to him. Ever notice your friend that is only around when she's not in a relationship or when her relationship is on its last leg? Don't be that friend. People don't like to feel used. Once your girlfriends realize you are only conveniently around when your man isn't, they won't want to be around you altogether. There is nothing wrong with having friendships with others. In fact, they are beneficial and make for healthier relationships. Why? Remember absence makes the heart grow fonder.

Couples need time apart. Time away should not be one sided. You should be able to do things together, with mutual friends, and alone. Guys hang out with the boys whenever they get ready to; so do what makes you happy. They do not forget Monday night football with Roy, or yearly fishing trips; so, go have Girls Night Out and Spa Days. You were an individual before you became a couple and "Me Time" is your entitlement.

Play Five

Be Independent

There is no wonder male rap and R&B artists write songs about independent women. There is nothing sexier than a woman that can take care of herself, not needing to rely on others for monetary support. Being financially free will not only give you higher self esteem; but, others will have greater respect for you as well.

Play Five, First Down

Don't take money for something a price can't be put on.

You have to trust yourself and your abilities. I'm sure every woman has many talents that go beyond those performed in the bedroom. I'm not saying there is something wrong with the man you're seeing helping you financially or buying you things. There is something to be said for a man who wants to see his woman doing well and looking good therefore giving freely.

When others feel you need them, they begin to feel a sense of control over you. You begin to accept things you wouldn't normally, because of this shift in power. You must at all times **remain in possession of your power**! If your partner helps you with your bills be sure that he knows, undoubtedly, your bills will be paid with or without his help.

If you happen to be a housewife or girlfriend whose arrangement does not consist of working or contributing financially, it is important that you still obtain options or unconventional methods of earning some money of your own no matter how large or small. Remember how frustrating it was as a child to have to ask your parents for everything you wanted? You knew that if you asked for a new pair of jeans, you wouldn't get them if your grades or chores hadn't been kept up. A man will hang things over your head for leverage just as your parents did. What grown woman wants to have to ask her partner for every little thing she needs? *Baby, I ran out of tampons; can I have five dollars?* Grown women should have their own pocket change, if nothing else. Perhaps you have a trust fund, a home business- doing hair at the kitchen sink, sell prepaid legal, Mary Kay®, or Body Magic®. Whatever the case may be, ensure you have a means for an out; or you may find yourself sticking around in an unhealthy relationship.

There was a time when I was in an unhealthy relationship while working an underpaid job. My partner was a habitual liar and cheater. I was unhappy in the relationship, but felt stuck because of the financial support I received, and needed, due to the slack in my own paycheck. Eventually, I came to the realization that I loved myself far too much to remain in a situation which was not beneficial to my own emotional stability. I realized there was no amount of money worth my self-pride. I stopped sitting around idle, relying on him financially. I found a job that allowed me to pick up my own slack, and then some. Needless to say, he is a thing of the past, and my self-esteem, is still in tack.

As little girls some of us were taught to rely on others because we are these precious, fragile, little beings, unable to support ourselves. As adults, we have to convince ourselves that we can do and be anything we set our minds to. We don't have to do anything for money that makes us feel uncomfortable or ashamed. I believe no one should do anything in private they'd be ashamed of if others found out. Tests present themselves in our lives; and, it is up to us to have the belief that God will see us through our struggles, if only we have the faith of a mustard seed.

Play Five, Second Down

Plan ahead for stormy weather.

Think smart before giving up your living arrangements to move in with a man. Make sure you have a nest egg put away for rainy days. Let's face it; relationships don't always weather the storm. Your nest egg may also be considered your rest egg. It is a way for you to rest assured that if something goes wrong you can easily make things right. Ensure you have enough money tucked away for moving expenses, security deposit, first and second months rent, and utilities. You never know when a relationship may turn sour and you'll need to make a speedy getaway.

Remember not to use your nest egg as leverage, throwing it in his face every chance you get. You do not have to tell him I have money saved and I can leave at the drop of a dime. Doing so, leaves a person feeling unstable and insecure, and makes for an unhealthy relationship.

Play Six

Be a Lady in the Streets

How often have you heard men say, "I want *a lady in the streets and a freak in the sheets?"* There is a reason this expression is so popularly quoted. We have forgotten how to let men take on the masculine role while we enjoy their efforts due to our attractive feminine qualities. This does not at all mean be docile, timid, and meek. But always, at all times, speak, look, and act, like a lady.

Play Six, First Down

A lady does not have the mouth of a sailor.

We do not have to strive to be June Cleaver; but in today's day and age we can definitely hold intelligent conversations without the excessive use of profanities. Spitting curse words and vulgarities out of your mouth every other statement is not attractive and draws negative attention. Men are attracted to and admire pouty mouths not potty mouths.

More often than not when a man chooses his partner he is not looking for someone who reminds him of one of the boys. Yes, he wants to be able to hang out and have fun with you. But he also wants a lady. He doesn't want someone he's embarrassed to bring around the guys because he doesn't know what may come out of her mouth. He doesn't want someone so loud and obnoxious when in public others are embarrassed for him.

There are times when you can let your hair down and hang loose. There couldn't be a better time than when the girls get together for girls night. I'm sure we can all relate to your womanly issues and wouldn't mind lending an ear to listen while you vent.

Play Six, Second Down

A lady expects chivalry.

What this means is that your king treats you like a queen. You are not incompetent, but you do have standards. Your standards should suggest you are worthy of being treated like a lady. A lady waits at a closed door until it is opened and stands at her chair until it is pulled out for her. Be sure to be courteous, saying please, and thank you, for his efforts. Let a gentlemen know his actions are not unrecognized or unappreciated. Doing so will encourage him to continue his chivalrous behavior. Men treat the women they care for with respect. If he doesn't know how to treat you, teach him. In turn, he'll have more respect for you.

Play Six, Third Down

Do not drink publicly, until intoxicated and pissy drunk.

Too much alcohol has a way of making us say and do things we wouldn't normally do and say. At these times we leave ourselves open, out of our comfort zone, and off our square. Believe me, there is nothing cute about using the bathroom on yourself or anywhere in public. There is nothing funny about you waking, and not remembering what you did the night before, how you got home, or who is lying beside you.

Trust me I have plenty of embarrassing drunk stories. But with growth came the realization that while intoxicated I was not representing the true me. I don't want to hear about what happened the previous night by others because I don't remember. I wish to be in control of my actions at all times.

There is nothing wrong with having a cocktail; but, learn to control your intake. Order fruit juices, wine, or something light and girly that won't have you falling off bar stools by the end of the night. Fruit juices are healthier, and leave you feeling rejuvenated and refreshed in the morning instead of fatigued and sluggish. Wine, often takes longer to have an effect and looks more sophisticated and lady like. Other girlish drinks which aren't as strong and won't put hair on your chest include Malibu and pineapple juice, Midori sour, and Daiquiri's. Be sure when you are out having drinks, you are with others that have your best interests in mind. Your true friends won't let you do things drunk they know you wouldn't do sober.

Play Six, Fourth Down

Always look the par.

Remember, everyday is game day, so always be prepared. A lady dresses and fixes herself up in a manner that accentuates her feminine qualities. Take pride in your appearance. Create the brand, "YOU." Find a look that works well for you and own it. It doesn't matter if it's Sassy Chic, Sexy Sleek, or Bohemian Geek.

Always groom yourself before leaving the house because you never know who you're going to run into. Steer clear of having to duck and dodge behind counter tops and signs trying to avoid running into an old school mate, beau, or crush because you're not looking your best. Even if you don't run into anyone, you never know who is watching you. Always create the best possible impression.

Game Day Dress Code

Don't...

...wear pajamas or house shoes in public

...wear clothes two sizes too big or too small, looking like a busted can of biscuits

...show too much skin, leaving nothing to the imagination

...dress sloppily, wrinkled, and worn out

. ..belch aloud and or pass gas, purposely in public

Do....

...maintain good personal hygiene

...wear proper undergarments

...dress and act your age

...dress for the occasion

...comb your hair, before leaving the house

...*Pass* to your daughter, through words and by example, all things a lady does and does not do

Men enjoy our feminine abilities, so by all means, use them to your advantage. A man once told me his biggest turn on was for a woman to be seated, wearing a dress or skirt, and take one of her thighs and cross it over the other. Who knew something so innocent and thoughtless could be such a major turn on? Therefore, look and act like a lady; and reap the benefits. Sure, he may still want to sleep with the trashy type. But like trash, she must leave in the wee hours of the morning, while things worth keeping, are put on display and cherished.

Play Seven

Close Your Legs

"**D**o not give what is holy to dogs, and do not throw pearls before swine, lest they trample them under their feet, and turn and tear you to pieces." (Matthew 7:6)

Play Seven, First Down

Make him wait.

A great many women believe their power lies between their legs, thus performing *loose ball fouls* and *free throwing*. They meet a man; and, after one encounter say to themselves, this man is everything I want and need. I got that good, good; and, I know just how to lay it down. So, for the next greeting she invites him over, spends all *her* grocery money making *his* favorite meal, and proceeds to put her best foot and head forward to get her man.

Question: Why on earth if you had the power did you give it to him? He is someone you barely know and who hardly knows you. Why would you expect him to want to stick around for more than round two or three? You have already shown him your best hand. He does not need to stick around. Think. When playing a game of spades, is the game not more interesting when you hold on to the Joker or Trump until towards the end of the game? When you go to work everyday, put in over time and save to buy a much wanted item like a diamond tennis bracelet, don't you appreciate it far greater than had it been handed to you as if it was something that comes a dime a dozen? Men think no differently; what's easily gotten is easily forgotten. The harder he has to work for something the more appreciative he is once he finally receives it.

How many times have you thought this is the one because in the very beginning everything was going great? On the second or third date perhaps sooner, you *free throw*. Three weeks into the relationship or situation *(whichever you choose to call it)* you begin to realize this person is not at all someone you wish to be with. Had you waited, this revelation would have been realized beforehand. People have a tendency to eventually show you who they really are no matter the initial front. It is your job to take your time and get to know someone such that this process takes place before your heart, pride, and panties are on the line.   It is your responsibility to ensure you aren't *free throwing* when it comes to having sex.

Perhaps something broader, deeper, and more meaningful, could have materialized had you waited to let him tap that. I am a firm believer that women have all the power **before** lying down with a man. This is so because men think with their small heads and women think with their hearts. For women it is difficult to not become emotionally attached after having slept with a guy. The longer you wait to sleep with a man the more you get to know him, and the more time passes. Later he thinks of you, he is not only thinking with his small head but also with the big one on top of his shoulders.

I personally believe waiting to have sex until marriage is a beautiful commitment which is how God intended it be. But let's face it. Most people don't choose to wait until marriage before giving so freely of themselves. I do not have a magic number of dates or three month rule which women should adhere to. If your ultimate goal is a serious committed relationship, waiting to have sex until the man really knows who you are, (and actually cares about you not the possibility of what you can do for him in the bedroom) is probably the single most important thing you can do.

When it is time, I believe that you will know and feel it in your gut, which speaks more clearly to you than your heart, which will let you know when it is okay to sleep with the man in which you are in a committed, monogamous, relationship with. Be mindful that commitment does not happen over the weekend or in two weeks unless you are in junior high. Rome wasn't built in a day and neither are solid relationships. Take your time and form strong relationships with foundation that can not be easily disrupted.

Oftentimes we choose to rationalize having sex without commitment with such excuses as, "*I want to test the waters first to see what I'm getting myself into. I have needs; there is no reason I can't have my needs fulfilled while I'm waiting for my future whatever to come along."* Ladies, we have to give ourselves more credit. We as women are probably the most resourceful species on this planet. We have been conditioned to go and do without so much that by now it is probably a part of our genetic makeup.

In the past, we had to cope without voting rights, equal salaries, and higher dry cleaning bills. What have we done? We fought for voting rights, while simultaneously managing to pay all our bills, wear clean clothes, put food in our mouths, and still buy new shoes. With today's technology, bullets, and rabbits I'm sure we can overcome a temporary need which can be easily fulfilled on our own.

Besides, something begins to happen internally the longer you go without needing another person to fill this void. You begin to become stronger emotionally. You give off an aura that is attractive to men because it is an aura of power and not like one of the dwarf's needy, easy, or sleazy.

Time Out:

Just to let you know, because some of us do tend to forget from time to time, or perhaps, some of us have never even known, that what's between your legs is priceless. It's the highest prize you have, the only one you're ever going to have and you must treat it as such if you ever expect a man to do the same.

Resume Play

I believe there is power and support in numbers. For those wishing to wait and endure, wear a string of pearls symbolizing your commitment to keep your virginity or as a vow of celibacy. *Pass* to your daughters, sisters, nieces, and neighbors the importance of saving themselves. Educate them on their value and worth. It is time we stop taking irresponsible chances with our bodies. A woman of power knows her worth; and, worth begins to decrease if it is not at its healthiest.

Based on research, over two million sexually active people transmit Chlamydia each year. Gonorrhea seems to be the gift that keeps on giving, as nearly 700,000 persons per year receive it. One in every five people has genital herpes, and in 2006 and 2007 combined there were over one million reported new cases of h.i.v infection in Americans.

Play Seven, Second Down

Before sex, go see the doctor!

If you are ashamed or embarrassed to ask him to go for a check-up, then you aren't ready to sleep with him. There is nothing you shouldn't be able to ask someone who you are willing to share something so intimate, sacred, and personal, as your body with. If he will not go, don't sleep with him; he has something to hide. A man with nothing to hide should delight in the fact that the woman he wishes to be with respects herself enough to want to protect herself. A responsible man will want the same sense of protection as well.

Like a mother lion protects her cub, we are queens, and must protect our jewels. We must not be so trusting with our *Precious Pearls*. I remember going to the clinic to have h.i.v testing. There were three others being tested that day. An older woman, a middle aged man- accompanied by his girlfriend (*who was not being tested*), a teenage girl, and myself. We were tested in this same order. The phlebotomist called us individually. During my test he pricked my finger and placed a small amount of blood on litmus paper, placed the sheet inside a tube, and put my tube inside a tray with the three previous tests. During this time he sparked conversation with me concerning the importance of being tested, having your partner tested, and accompanying him inside the room where the test is taking place, in my case of a 30 minute same day result. There is no paperwork accompanying this sort of test. The phlebotomist explained, far too often, couples will come in to be tested, the woman will receive hers then return to the waiting area. The guy will proceed to inform the phlebotomist he does not need to be tested because he has already received positive results unbeknown to his partner.

While waiting for my results the older woman received hers and left. Upon returning from the conference room the middle aged man, wearing a broad smile, came out, and immediately told his girlfriend he was straight *(meaning he was negative)*. Anxious and nervous I went to the bathroom and soon after returned. Upon returning I smiled at the young girl as she was gathering her things to leave the waiting area. She smiled back saying, "You must be negative like me." I told her I hadn't received my results yet. Just then my number was called, number four. I went into the conference room. The phlebotomist brought over the tray with all four tubes. He faced them towards me, pointing to the first two tests explained, "The red mark indicates a positive result." Now, pointing to the last two tubes, he said, "The lack of color on these two, indicate negative results. Your test is negative." Needless to say I was relieved beyond belief.

After leaving the doctor's office you would have thought my mind would be totally clear and at ease, but it wasn't. I couldn't stop thinking about the two positive results that preceded the teenage girl and my negative results. What not only boggled but also angered me was the bold faced lie the middle aged man walked out and told his girlfriend, wearing the broad smile of a professional schemer, liar, and murderer. The moral of this story which should go without saying is, DO NOT TRUST **ANYONE** WITH YOUR LIFE!!!

H.I.V./AIDS is one of the most widely hidden and highly ostracized infections, especially in the African American community. I believe the widespread negative attention persons carrying this disease receive is because the majority of us are uneducated. If those carrying the virus felt less ostracized and accepted, the likelihood of them feeling more comfortable in sharing their status would increase. In turn, newly infected cases, would decrease.

Recently, I heard a story of a girl who was upset because she smoked a "funny cigarette" behind another young lady said to be infected with the virus. She stated she felt violated and that her options had been taken away. It is amazing to me how people can make blind, ridiculous, and totally asinine statements such as this, yet willingly lay down with a man and have unprotected sex. Ignorance must be bliss to make a person do and say such a thing as this. Take time and educate yourself on facts concerning transmission!

Play Eight

Don't Eat Forbidden Fruit

Borrow your girlfriend's shoes. Borrow your sisters black clutch that goes with your black skinny jeans. You may even choose to go on a website such as Bag Borrow or Steal©, purchase loaned handbags, use them until you're through, then share them with someone else. But do not, under any circumstances whatsoever, bed, a borrowed, or shared man.

Play Eight, First Down

Don't play the game with married and attached men.

Contrary to popular belief, there are more than enough men to go around. Live by the motto, "More Than Enough." There is more than enough of everything needed for everyone to survive, this includes men. Again, the idealist in me does not believe all black men are jobless, gay, on the down low, already in relationships, with white women, or in jail. Rather you are looking for as a popular neo soul artist put it, your Wall Street brother or your down for whatever chilling on the corner brother, you must locate your own.

An older well established man I'd been seeing once told me he was stunned beyond belief that he was being rejected by a younger woman because of his temporary situation *(That being his involvement with another woman).* The reason he was stunned is because so many times we allow men to come into our lives attached, having not completely ended an already failing relationship. If the relationship is failing, let it fail. After it has ended and the threat of becoming his rebound or baggage handler has passed, then perhaps a flame can be sparked.

There is no need to try and build a friendship with this man. His proposed harmless friendship, is also his way of finagling his way into your life despite your already stated opposition to his situation. This is the exact wrong thing to do, especially when you find this man attractive.

What you are doing, is making a difficult situation worse. It is complicated and next to impossible for men and women who find each other attractive to remain platonic. I'm sure you've heard the saying, do unto others as you would have others do unto you. If you wouldn't want your spouse to secretly befriend women, then don't secretly befriend married and attached men. Besides, we all know nothing strictly innocent needs to be kept a secret or hidden.

Why on earth would you choose a piece of a man when you can have a whole man of your own?

There is no reason to continue to live with your eyes wide shut and your legs wide open. Men only do as much as we allow them to get away with. If we choose not to sleep with attached men they can not continue to cheat, bottom line. No matter what you tell yourself *(if it wasn't me it'd be somebody else; I'm doing her a favor; it's only temporary; fair exchange ain't robbery; yada, yada, yada)* you cannot put a Cadillac emblem on a Neon and call it a Cadillac. It is still a Dodge Neon. Likewise, you cannot put justification on wrong and call it right. It is still wrong.

In the end, the woman choosing to sleep with another woman's husband or boyfriend ends up alone and lonely. Most men never leave the relationship. Why should he when he can continue to have his cake and eat you too? On the rare occasion he does leave home, he repeats similar behavior in your relationship; or, you ruin what could have been because of paranoia from the boomerang effect. What you do to others comes back to you.

When you knowingly do wrong, you block your own blessings. Although you may seem to benefit outwardly in the beginning, your wrong doings never fail to catch up with you. Ironically, pay back does not always occur in the same manner you paid it. Unlike loaned money, karma tends to pay you back at least twice as great.

Everything we were taught, be it spoken, or learned behavior, is not necessarily best. I know a woman, let's call her Angela, whose mother for many years tirelessly wore herself thin trying to *intercept* a married man (Angela's father) until he finally gave her the boot and recommitted himself to his wife and family. Angela now mimics this same learned behavior, chasing countless unattainable men as if it were a sport. Our mothers did the best they knew to do, but again, we must end generational curses or continue to suffer from their ever existing prowess.

Honestly speaking, at some time in all our lives we have all been affected by a cheating man. It is not a good feeling whether you are on the receiving or giving end of the devious activity. I don't care what you try telling yourself. You deserve a man who is deserving of you. Recognize a *brick* when you see it and leave. Remember, a deserving man will not hurt you in such a manner that tears you down and wipes away your self-esteem.

Simply put, no when to hold em' and no when to fold em'. You should be able to be in a relationship and trust your partner. Nothing beneficial comes from remaining in a relationship where trust has been lost. Who benefits from you waiting until he falls asleep so that you may check his phone log or text messages? Who benefits from you following and stalking a man who you share so you may bust the windows out of his car? Who benefits from the countless arguments and accusations of what is undeniably occurring, whether a confession or caught in the act is attained?

Snooping is a sign of insecurity and an unhealthy relationship. It is cancerous and highly consumable. People often start off small by reading a note left behind on the table or forgotten in a jacket pocket. Then, the snooping matriculates into looking through phones, breaking email codes, and checking voice mails. It becomes a habit that will consume you. You'll find yourself playing sleep until he dozes off so you can pry through his things. Even when nothing is found, snooping hardly ever stops until it blows up in the offenders face. However difficult, bottom line is, don't start something that you know rarely ever has a happy ending.

Stalking is a sign of an unhealthy person. Hiding behind bushes and trash cans are not healthy behaviors. Most often a person is being stalked because they want nothing to do with the stalker. Accept that if someone doesn't want a relationship with you following them around town will not change their mind. In fact, if they didn't want you before, they definitely won't want you if they find out stalking is how you've been spending your spare time.

Matters of the heart are difficult to get over. During break ups are ideal times to practice being strong. Everyone has their own way of coping with difficult situations, but be sure to find a healthy outlet such as prayer, leaning on friends, or momentarily staying away from things that remind you of the person. Whatever the case, remember that with time heartache becomes easier to manage.

I have a friend that created a star chart as a way of getting over her ex. At the end of each day, if she had successfully not driven by his home, called his phone, or checked his Facebook® status, she'd give herself a star. After ten stars she'd treat herself to something nice. As time went by she found she no longer needed the chart at all. Her remedy for a broken heart may be a little far fetched for some. Whatever the case may be, find a positive way to deal with your breakup.

There is no reason to moonlight as an undercover detective. What's done in the dark will eventually come to light. Let us practice using the sense God gave us, the detective skills and thought process used when trying to catch a cheating man, when not believing every cover up, lie, and lame excuse, thrown our way.

- If you have never been to your man's house, he is not your man.

- If he is never around on holidays or special occasions, you are certainly not number one.

- As my Great Grandmother would say, *"Don't nothing take all night."* The only thing open all night are legs. Therefore, there is never a good enough excuse for him to spend the night out.

- A single man with no children does not purchase a mini van.

- He did not *mysteriously* miss all your calls; your call did not *miraculously* go to voicemail after the first ring, and his phone was not *mistakenly* turned off all night.

- There is no reason or excuse good enough for him to not formally break a date. If he had enough time to make a date, he has enough time to break a date.

- If you are still waiting on him dressed and ready to go an hour after his supposed arrival, and have not received a courtesy call, there is no need to waste a perfectly good outfit and hairdo. Pick up your keys and go out without him. *(Yes, this applies to street hustlers as well.)*

- Hickeys are not rashes or insect bites, and are only formed by a human mouth making suction on the reddened area.

- He did not catch crabs or any other s.t.d. from a toilet seat or a stripper sitting on his lap.

- If it looks and behaves as a dog it probably is just that. There is no need to bring it home and try to house break it. Besides, it probably has fleas, in which case you'll want to stay far away.

Cheating shall not be tolerated. If your partner has cheated it is best to leave the relationship. It is unhealthy. Like puppies and children, men learn from mistakes when consequences follow misbehavior. Typically, people don't totally learn lessons until *penalties* have been paid. I know it is difficult to leave a relationship when feelings, children, and vows are involved. I am not saying relationships can't recover from infidelity but boundaries must be reestablished before reentering the relationship or he will never take you seriously and the same behaviors will repeat themselves.

When you separate, you must totally cut him off as much as possible. This may be difficult when children are involved. But there is a difference between cutting him off from you and cutting him off from his children. When you don't let your children see their father, you hurt your children the most. Often times, as they get older they only end up resenting you. It doesn't matter how badly your child's father has treated you. If you don't feel your child is in danger being with his father, don't come between their relationship. How he treated you is what he did to you, and most often, what you allowed him to do to you; don't punish your child for it. If dad is really a jerk your children will find this out in their own time and form their own opinion of their father.

Remember, you cannot be friends with someone who misuses your trust. You most definitely cannot sleep with him. Misbehavior should not be rewarded. Do not *fumble* and commit a *loose ball foul*. Why would you break up with someone for cheating on you and in turn reward him with sex; no strings attached, no commitment, no *penalty*, or responsibility to you? Doing so sends the wrong message. The message being sent is, it is okay to do whatever you choose to me because I will always be around. Not to mention, you give him no reason to fix his behavior because now he has you in an even better position than before.

Always *lay up* and *assist* your teammates. Women must stick together if we ever want to win the game. We as women must have morals and standards or we will continue to be stuck in the same rut. Morals help us discern between what looks and feels good, but is bad for us. There is no written code of ethics for who is off limits when dating, but if there were, it would read as follows:

<u>Women's Off Limits Code of Ethics</u>

1. Do not date or sleep with someone any family member has dated or slept with, no matter how distant the relation, or long ago the encounter. These situations do not have expiration dates. Doing so will leave a guaranteed sour taste in someone's mouth.

2. Do not date or sleep with any man a friend has gone on a date with or slept with. Hint: *A friend is another woman you talk to and or hang out with at least once a year.*

3. Do not date more than one person per job, neighborhood, school, church, organization etc. without leaving at least a two year window between encounters. If you find this difficult you are not getting out enough. You need to broaden your circle.

4. Do not accept an invitation to dinner or bed from your ex's friend, relative, co-worker or close associate.

5. No matter the men, do not sleep with more than one, per ovulation cycle. We must not continue to make appearances on talk shows to find out who our baby daddies are. Doing so gives every one of us a bad rep.

Victory

Game Recognized

Now that we know what we've all done wrong, let's laugh at ourselves for allowing this utterly ridiculous behavior to take place. After going to the bathroom, wiping away your tears of laughter, sorrow, or regret, and calling your closest girlfriend, come right back so we may begin the process of CHANGE.

Before moving ahead you must learn the power of forgiveness. You must learn to forgive yourself and others for past mistakes. Forgive others of their past wrong doings no matter the misdeed because there is power in forgiveness. In order to totally heal, you must forgive all those who have ever done you wrong.

This includes forgiving those who have cursed you generationally, scheming friends and acquaintances, cheating exes, and lying spouses. Reach deep and forgive those that have disappointed you by leaving you hollow and torn on the inside unable to face reality. Forgive those who have left lasting impressions and hopes for a future only to disappear abruptly leaving you disappointed, misled, and confused. Let go of every grudge, sense of resentment, cold shoulder and shoulder chip.

You don't have to try to get people back for their wrong doings. Doing so is petty. It shows a lack of maturity as well as you care and there are still lingering feelings. Let it all go because now you can finally breathe, spread your wings, and fly. You are finally free! You are finally free to do you and be the best you possible.

You no longer have to act as though you are blind and don't see what's directly in front of you. You now realize the power you possess is strong and through that strength you can stand up for yourself. You now expect more of yourself and others. You can set good examples for those watching you and looking up to you. You can confidently tell someone when they are treating you in a manner you wish not be treated; and, know it is his lost if he doesn't correct his actions immediately because you will not stick around and tolerate misbehavior.

With all that being said, and although you know you are a Queen and expect only the best, inevitably times can and will get tough. Difficult situations and trying obstacles will present themselves. During those times you must remain stead strong and endure the test. You might slip up and fall back into some of your old ways. There might be times you find yourself falling into your former habits. Don't beat yourself up about it. Recognize the slip up right away; and, fix it right away. The old sayings are true. It's hard to teach an old dog new trick's; but practice does make perfect.

Remember, be strong. Pray and find inspiration when times get tough. There is a pot of gold at the end of the rainbow. I and others like me have made it to the game. We're cheering for you and rooting you on. So lace up your running shoes and get ready to win the race. Let's let men know we came prepared. We're all playing on the same team. We got our game face on, and we will, we will, rock you!

GLOSSARY

1. **Airball** *(noun)-* similar to an airhead, a woman who is unable to take a hint or clue; commonly these women are also hackers

2. **Assist** *(verb)-* the offering of help and support from one woman to the next in any number of ways

3. **Brick** *(adjective)-* An unsuccessful date, relationship or ugly breakup; basically, nothing about the situation went well

4. **Flagrant Foul** *(adjective)-* an extremely offensive dating "don't" has taken place

5. **Free Throw** *(verb)-* to have sex with no strings attached

6. **Hack** *(verb)* - to overcompensate or chase someone of the opposite sex who isn't reciprocating interest

7. **Interception** *(verb)-* when a man has been taken or stolen from one woman by another

8. **Lay Up** *(verb)*- When someone who has your best interest at heart informs you of your shortcomings or downfalls in your relationship

9. **Loose Ball Foul** *(verb)* - the act of having sex with an ex boyfriend or any undeserving individual

10. **Passing** *(verb)*- The responsibility older and wiser women have to the younger female generation of giving and handing down knowledge and game rules

11. **Penalty**- Consequence or repercussion paid for mistreatment

12. **Punt** *(verb)*- To give up or throw in the towel on an unsuccessful relationship

13. **Wide Receiver** *(noun)*- a woman with no morals therefore showing no respect for herself; commonly, these women are also loose ball foulers

Happy With Me Steps:

My man is...

Notes

Notes

A PERSONAL GUIDE FOR SELF REFLECTION

ABOUT THIS GUIDE:

The following questions are meant to improve your reading of Tanisha Brooks'

Woman to Woman: It's Time to Change the Game

The Play Book

Personal Guide for Self Reflection

1. Do you feel your being single has anything to do with the dating standards of today? Do you contribute to the destruction of, or enhance the mode of today's dating scene?

2. In what ways can you enhance your inner and outer beauty?

3. When in a relationship, do you often find yourself putting the needs of your partner before your own? In what ways is doing so a hindrance to your emotional well being? Do others complain of you being selfish, self centered or narcissistic? How has this behavior affected relationships?

4. Do you overlook what should be major deal breakers when choosing a partner? If so, why?

5. How soon is too soon...

    - To begin a relationship

    - To pay for a date

    - For intimacy

6. Do you tend to depend on others to provide things you should provide for yourself? Why? What steps can you take to reverse this role?

7. What are your unique feminine qualities? In what ways can you turn these qualities up or down to be considered "more ladylike and appealing?"

8. How often do you have unprotected sex? Why? Typically, do you and your partner go to the Dr. before becoming intimate? Typically, do you and your partner discuss opinions concerning marriage and parenting before becoming intimate?

9. Do you agree with the "Women's Off Limit Code of Ethics?" Which codes do you believe are most relevant? Which codes have you violated? Why?

10. Upon reading *The Play Book,* what will you change about you that most needs altering? In what ways will you *pass* essential plays to other young girls and women, in an effort to change the game?

Author's Bio

Tanisha Brooks grew up in Chicago Illinois. She received her BBA from Robert Morris University. She is currently in pursuit of her MAED from the University of Phoenix while consecutively working as an elementary school teacher. Throughout her adult life many have recognized her talent as a writer and poet and have encouraged her to publish her works. As life inevitably occurs others outlook for her future has become her own and so she writes her first book, *Woman to Woman: It's Time to Change the Game.* Tanisha may be reached by writing her personally at game_recognized@yahoo.com or by visiting her web page at www.tanishabrooks.net

www.ingramcontent.com/pod-product-compliance
Lightning Source LLC
Chambersburg PA
CBHW072026040426
42447CB00009B/1746